# The Fast Of The Lord

Walter Crawford

© 2013 Walter Crawford

All Rights Reserved

## ISAIAH 58
## THE FAST OF THE LORD

Each time I refresh myself in the reading of this chapter, I discover fresh manna. Although I have read it many times as an anchor of my personal development in the Lord, there is always something new and refining in fresh revelation of what God requires of us in prayer and fasting.

There is a popular Christian belief that by prayer and fasting we can invoke the ear of God to extend His hand to grant the prayers petitioned in our requests. Aligned with this thinking is the popular belief that by sheer weight of numbers God will be moved to answer those participating in the operation. Though these be worthy ideals in the natural, God does not operate in such an arena. One individual humbled before God can experience powerful results, as God has settled His Word in heaven and is fulfilling His Word upon the earth. (Example: Ahab humbled himself and God held back judgment.)

The opening verses of this chapter initially indicate that our concept of transgression and sin is entirely different from how God views them. Man concludes and judges from external moral standards; whereas God, who sees the deep intent of the heart, because of His established Word will respond in accordance to His declaration of that Word.

Verses 1-2: Cry aloud, spare not, lift up thy voice like a trumpet, and shew My people their transgression (rebellion), and the house of Jacob their sins. Yet they seek Me daily, and delight to know My ways, as a nation that did righteousness, and forsook not the ordinance of their God: they ask of Me the ordinances of justice; they take delight in approaching to God.

Initially these verses would seem highly commendable. Yet as we read further, we will discover motivation and agendas which are not acceptable to the Lord.

ISAIAH 58:3-5.
THE FAST OF THE LORD (Part 2)

In my spirit I have always related this chapter to the teaching of Jesus in MATTHEW--CHAPTERS 5, 6, & 7. Both draw our attention to the need for pure heart expression in our relationship with the Lord and each other, which is pleasing and acceptable to God our Father and our Lord and Savior Jesus Christ. Today, as in the day of Isaiah, we have become more attentive to religious ceremony and evangelical escapism than to the undefiled practical and sacrificial teaching of Jesus. We have majored in the personality of Christ to the near exclusion of His message.

Many continue to strive for the message of Moses and have made it the measure stick, only validating Jesus as a means of salvation. Sadly, our actions and way of life have neither produced fruit for the Lesser Law of Moses or the Higher Law of Jesus. Some have stated that the teaching of Jesus is impossible to achieve. Yet the Holy Spirit was given at Pentecost as the Enabler, giving us the Spiritual energy to become the wo/men that God desired Adam/Eve to be from the beginning, overcomers with the Spiritual authority to 'Till the Ground'. (Implied here is the thought of us cultivating each other...in short, being our brother's keeper!) Religious ostentation has replaced true Spiritual values, and in Isaiah an angry people berate God for failing to answer their fasting and prayers.

VERSES 3-5: (The people's question) Wherefore have we fasted, say they, and Thou seest not? Wherefore have we afflicted our soul, and Thou takest no knowledge? (God's answer) Behold, in the day of your fast ye find pleasure, and exact all your labours. Behold, ye fast for strife and debate, and to smite with the fist of wickedness: ye shall not fast as ye do this day, to make your voice to be heard on high. Is it such a fast that I have chosen? A day for a man to afflict his soul? Is it to bow down his head as a bulrush, and to spread sackcloth and ashes under him? Wilt thou call this a fast, and an acceptable day to the Lord?

Individually we must ask the Holy Spirit to interpret this and show us what it means to each of us.

ISAIAH 58: 6-7
THE FAST OF THE LORD (Part 3)

It's ironical that what we think constitutes fasting and prayer is contrary to what God recognizes and responds to as we earnestly seek to fulfill His will in our lives. The following is a recipe for immediate 'then' results from God:

Is not this the fast that I have chosen?
To loose the bands of wickedness,
To undo the heavy burdens,
And to let the oppressed go free,
And that YE...YE...YOU break every yoke?
Is it not to deal thy bread to the hungry,
And that thou bring the poor that are cast out to thy house?
When thou seest the naked, that thou cover him;
AND THAT THOU HIDE NOT THYSELF FROM THINE OWN FLESH?

Eight awesome requirements given by God for an automatic spiritual response from heaven! Some of you may have already attained to these lofty ideals in your spiritual growth and are reaping the beautiful benefits. Some, like me, are still struggling as we aspire to attain by accepting our responsibility for our previous and present failures by acknowledging the Truth of God's Word.

Tomorrow the glorious results of the THEN, THEN, THEN of God!

ISAIAH 58:8-9.
THE FAST OF THE LORD (Part 4)

When I went to school I wasn't too bright, but I did do well in geometry. We were given a statement concerning a theory, with a formula which we then had to prove with an extension. So after the proper application we would conclude with THEN.....

In the previous two verses God has given us a formula for revival by His application of prayer and fasting, which if we apply in our daily living, THEN, THEN, THEN we will experience the glorious results of 'The Fast of the Lord!'

THEN shall thy light break forth as the morning, and thine HEALTH shall spring forth speedily: and thy righteousness shall go before thee; the glory of the Lord shall be thy rereward. THEN shalt thou call, and the Lord shall answer; thou shalt cry, and He shall say, Here I am. If thou take away from the midst of thee the yoke, the putting forth of the finger, and speaking vanity.

God has no pleasure in sackcloth and ashes, which are often no more than an extension of the vanity within us. His desire is that we treat each other with respect and dignity, which is the unadulterated teaching of Jesus. When our brother or sister is being maligned by unhealthy gossip, which often is fabricated lies, may we be the first to come to their defense by covering their nakedness, and refraining from the putting forth of the finger.

As we apply this in our lives, Divine Healing will begin to flow through our being.....or God is a liar!!

ISAIAH 58: 10-11
THE FAST OF THE LORD (Part 5)

When we apply ourselves to do things God's way even though externally things may be grave, internally we can have the peace of God which passeth all understanding; and in His Gracious Love and Mercy as we do it His way, all our paths become paths of pleasantness. In verses 10-11 God goes on to give us an added bonus by promises that each of us yearn for deep in our soul:

And if thou draw out thy soul to the hungry, and satisfy the afflicted soul; THEN shall thy light rise in obscurity, and thy darkness be as the noon day: And the Lord shall guide thee continually, and satisfy thy soul in drought, and make fat thy bones: and thou shalt be like a watered garden, and like a spring of water, whose waters fail not.

As I wrote the above scriptures, I could feel the Spirit move within me at the wonderful provision of God. Are not all these promises the very things we desire to become? Are not these promises the very aspirations that have eluded us in our quest through the medium of materialism as we sought to acquire 'toys and things'?

Let us again refresh ourselves with what God requires of us in order to obtain His favor. In fact, let us put to test His Word by a simple experiment: Each of us who has a problem with that insidious affliction of spontaneous gossiping (which is the pointing of the finger) determine for a day just for starters that I will not pass on gossip or speak words of presumptuous sins about my brother or sister. These are the 'pointing of the finger'.

Let us allow the Holy Spirit to keep us aware of how insidious these are because they are very prevalent in our thought life. May we think beautiful, positive things about each other instead of all the negativity that prevails as much in the churches as in the world. Try it for a day and you will sleep better at night, and the HEALTH OF THE LORD WILL FLOOD YOUR BEING!


ISAIAH 58:12
THE FAST OF THE LORD (Part 6)

For many years this has progressively become one of the most fascinating verses to me. As we begin to promote the Fast of the Lord revealed in the previous verses, the awesome revelation of our potential authority in the Spirit is quite amazing. At first I was hesitant to share what has been revealed to me, so I said "Lord, they will not understand!" The Lord replied, "You did!" It was then I realized that the Holy Spirit will reveal Truth to anyone who is hungry and desires to walk according to the Word.

And they that shall be of thee shall build the old waste places: thou shalt raise up the foundation of many generations; and thou shalt be called, The repairer of the breach, The restorer of paths to dwell in.

It is expedient for us to understand the initial Breach in order to move forward. I would suggest that when Adam/Eve ate of the Tree of Death (Tree of the Knowledge of Good and Evil) in Eden, allowing the headship of the serpent in their minds/souls, a BREACH or division (separation) was instigated between wo/man and God, which eventually led unrepentant wo/man to begin calling upon the name of the Lord. And to Seth, to him also there was born a son; and he called his name Enos: then began men to call upon the name of the LORD. (GENESIS 4: 26)

Unrepentant wo/man continued his/her downward spiral till God in His Gracious Love and Mercy came in the form of His beloved Son. By His death on the cross, Jesus laid the foundation whereby the horrible stench and filth of death, spewed out by the Tree of Death from Eden, not only could be contained, but that the retrograde action would be reversed and the plan of God fulfilled upon the earth.

The humbling thought in all of this is that you and I have been called to repair the breach by our hunger to live the

Fast of the Lord.

Now we can understand why Satan, active in the Ego of man, delights when we continue to kill one another with our tongues.


ISAIAH 58: 12
THE FAST OF THE LORD (Part 7)

As we allow the Holy Spirit to change our perspective from being self-centered to God-Conscious, awareness of the Fast of the Lord will become a way of life where our energies will not be focused on the 'Me', but rather on the spiritual restoration and redemption of mankind. I'm not referring to just the salvation message of the escapists, but the need of the application of the Fast of the Lord in bringing humanity in line with the mind of God in reclaiming that which was lost in Eden.

The thinking of the escapists is simply that they are going to be whisked off from earth to be cleaned up in heaven by some kind of 'magic passes' done by God. Then with Jesus they will return, empowered to rule and reign over cities. (We will never rule over cities if we cannot rule over ourselves!) These are worthy sentiments, yet it is the cleaning up process that is part of the Perfecting of the saints here on earth. And ye have forgotten the exhortation which speaketh unto you as children, MY SON, DESPISE

NOT THOU THE CHASTENING OF THE LORD, NOR FAINT WHEN THOU ART REBUKED OF HIM: FOR WHOM THE LORD LOVETH HE CHASTENETH, AND SCOURGETH EVERY SON WHOM HE RECEIVETH. If ye endure chastening, God dealeth with you as with sons; for what son is he whom the father chasteneth not? But if ye be without chastisement, whereof all are partakers, then are ye bastards, and not sons. (HEBREWS 12: 5-8)

If Jesus had to be Perfected through the things that He suffered to open the door for you and me to be glorified with Him, then the servant, being not greater than his Lord, should also expect the same discipline in order to become His disciple. Sadly many have entered into conflict with Satan rather than submit to the discipline of God.

The purpose of all this is that we may birth spiritual children who will be schooled and skilled to build. And they that shall be of thee shall build up the old waste places. Before we can build, we need to know what and where the old waste places are.

ISAIAH 58: 12
THE FAST OF THE LORD (Part 8)

We have already made reference to the Breach, which is the catalyst separating wo/man from God. Jesus at Calvary laid the foundation whereby you and I may, by our compliance to the Fast of the Lord and our re-birthed living, with our spiritual progenitors and spiritual descendants, Build the Old Waste Places. Let us seek by the Holy Spirit to interpret the Old Waste Places. First the word OLD in the Hebrew gives a more powerful vista than what we consider as OLD.

OLD: Hebrew, *OLAM*--To be concealed (i.e. the vanishing point), time out of mind (past or future), practically eternity. There are many more references to the meaning of this word OLD, but sufficient are the above for today without overwhelming our minds.

I have had the tendency to think that the VANISHING POINT of something is some place or time in the future; but as the scripture records the VANISHING POINT here, it is at the inception or beginning of the event. In this case the beginning of the event was our representatives' (Adam/Eve's) participation in the Tree of Death. This was the beginning of the literal/natural world and figurative/spiritual world becoming WASTE PLACES.

WASTE: Hebrew, *CHORBAH*--Drought, Desolation, Destruction, Decayed. I am sure all of us are agreed that these meanings well fit the condition and the deterioration of both the literal/natural and figurative/spiritual condition of this world since the eating of the Tree of Death in the Garden of Eden.

As I have said many times, since Adam/Eve did not take responsibility for their action, we also like them have the inherent reaction of placing the ultimate blame on the Serpent--Satan. One of the most powerful scriptures used in validating the DESOLATION and the fall of Satan is actually referencing a MAN as recorded in ISAIAH 14: 16-17 (Please read the whole chapter): They that see thee shall narrowly look upon thee, and consider thee, saying, IS THIS THE MAN that made the earth to tremble, that did shake kingdoms; that made the world as a wilderness, and destroyed the cities thereof; that opened not the house of his prisoners?

When each of us takes responsibility for our actions and reactions, allowing the Holy Spirit to deal with the deep-seated garbage within us handed down by generational curse, we will begin the REPAIRING OF THE BREACH...initially internally within us, then by example sowing the seeds of emancipation that others will also take up the challenge of REPAIRING THE BREACH.

ISAIAH 58: 13-14
THE FAST OF THE LORD (Part 9)

God initiated the Sabbath by the simple method of withholding the manna on the seventh day, which was to be a day of rest. Also it was meant as a day whereby wo/man could express their love and gratitude unto the Lord.

In the early church because of dissension between the Jews and the Christians, the Christians began to gather on the first day of the week, Sunday, instead of attending the synagogue on Saturday. Today there is still dissension between those who favor one day over the other. Sad to say, for too many in this materialistic age there is no Holy Day. It has become a time of pleasure promotion and work. This in itself has become another reason for the spiritual deterioration which undermines the foundation of the nation.

Having said that, there is a vast difference between the

Sabbath that Moses initiated (which is a type or shadow of the real) and the Sabbath of the Lord referred to in the above scriptures. In GENESIS 2: 2-3 God rested from all of His work: And on the seventh day God ended His work which He had made; and He rested on the seventh day from all His work which He had made. And God blessed the seventh day and sanctified it: because that in it He had rested from all His work which God created and made.

The word rested in the Hebrew is *SHABATH*. The difference between the sabbath of Moses and the sabbath of the Fast of the Lord in Isaiah, which is the *Shabath* of God in Genesis 2, is that the sabbath of Moses was/is a weekly intermission; whereas the sabbath of the Lord is an ongoing daily expression of the Life of Christ being exemplified in you and me. If we turn away from our own pleasure on God's Shabath (every day), and call the sabbath a delight, the holy of the Lord, honourable; and shalt honour Him, not doing thine own ways, nor finding thine own pleasure, nor speaking thine own words: THEN thou shalt delight thyself in the Lord; and I will cause thee to ride upon the high places of the earth, and feed thee with the heritage of Jacob thy father: for the mouth of the Lord hath spoken it.

ISAIAH 58
THE FAST OF THE LORD (Part 10)

It is expedient for each of us to realize that in the application of the precepts given by God in this chapter is the blueprint for healthy living. If we examine them closely we will conclude that, although these are necessities given by God, we can live in beautiful relationships both with God and mankind. Sadly these are not part of many 'church' programs. When last did we hear exhortations to:

Loose the bands of wickedness.
To undo the heavy burdens.
To let the oppressed go free.
Ye break every yoke.
Deal thy bread to the hungry.
Bring the poor that are cast out to thy house.
When thou seest the naked, that thou cover him.
And that thou hide not thyself from thine own flesh.
Take away from the midst of thee the yoke.
.....the putting forth of the finger.
.....speaking vanity.
Draw out thy soul to the hungry.
Satisfy the afflicted soul.

When we adopt these as a way of life, we are automatically covered by the 'THENS' of God.

We have been conditioned to believe that God does all these things, yet it is obvious that these are requirements of you and me as we seek to emulate the teaching of Jesus...which is so sadly neglected. In the next few lessons with the help of the Holy Spirit I will endeavor to elaborate on the above.

If this chapter gives God's recipe for Healthy Living and believers practice it, there wouldn't be the same need for a 'health bill' which also is Alternative Medicine!

ISAIAH 58: 6
THE FAST OF THE LORD (Part 11)

As Christians we have a responsibility to one another, which is actually our responsibility to God our Father. Even in the Lord's Prayer, which we are all so familiar with, Jesus makes it very evident that our forgiveness from Father is contingent on our forgiveness of each other. And forgive us our debts, AS WE FORGIVE our debtors.....For if ye forgive men their trespasses, your heavenly Father will also forgive you: But if ye FORGIVE NOT men their trespasses, neither will your Father forgive your trespasses. (MATTHEW 6: 12, 14-15)

Most of us at one time or other have had battles with unforgiveness. On one occasion, finding it difficult to forgive, the Lord made it quite clear to me that both my life and ministry would stagnate if I could not give true heart forgiveness. Also He made it quite evident that in our willingness to freely forgive lies the true evidence of

## one BEING BORN AGAIN!

Religions make their measure stick of salvation by the hypocritical keeping of their doctrinal DO'S and DON'TS. As we grow in the Lord and spiritually develop, there are many other essentials which contribute to HEALTHY LIVING both in the natural and in the spiritual. Such requirements are found in the FAST OF THE LORD, and today we will briefly look at verse 6. We have to loose the bands of wickedness, to undo the pain and fetters of moral iniquity. We have been conditioned to accept moral iniquity as the DO'S and DON'TS of religious persuasions, but it is much deeper than that. It is interesting to note the Living Bible interprets this scripture: No, the kind of fast I want is that you stop oppressing those who work for you and treat them fairly and give them what they earn. Because of his policies of taxation for his own pleasure, Solomon yoked the people to such painful bondage that it was the catalyst that ultimately divided the kingdom into Israel and Judah.

Today we have seen such displays of unparalleled greed by many without conscience that these moral iniquities stink to high heaven. The unsuspecting have been unscrupulously raped by the machinations of wicked men. Innocent, trusting people have lost their lifetime savings by such moral iniquity, turning their American dream into a nightmare.

Let it not be named of us, Beloved, that we also are partakers of such confusion. Rather let it be said that we are of those who have loosed the bands of wickedness. And thy righteousness shall go before thee, the glory of the Lord shall be thy rereward.

ISAIAH 58: 6
THE FAST OF THE LORD (Part 12)

It is very interesting how we easily use the Law of Moses when it is suitable to our purposes; and yet when the Law interferes with our plans, it is quickly discarded and pushed into the dark recesses of our minds. Jesus addressed this when He was talking to the scribes and Pharisees about their hypocrisy. Ye blind guides, which strain at a gnat, and swallow a camel....Even so ye also outwardly appear righteous unto men, but within ye are full of hypocrisy and iniquity. (Please read MATTHEW 23: 23-36) James 2: 10 also makes a profound statement: For whosoever shall keep the whole law, and yet offend in one point, he is guilty of all.

To appropriate the blessing of the Lord in the Fast of the Lord, it is expedient that we seek to fulfill the finer, smaller points which often we quickly read over thinking they don't count. Such points as to undo the heavy burdens, and to let the oppressed go free, and that ye break every yoke? We know that Jesus breaks the heavy yoke of the burden of sin of the oppressed sinner, yet there are moral obligations for us to fulfill in our relationships with our brothers and sisters.

In this day within the framework of Christianity many of the people are groaning under the yoke of building programs. Many are yoked and bound under great fear by unscrupulous hirelings whose intent is to shear the sheep, keeping them oppressed by conditioning them to painful repercussions if they fail in their Tithes and Offerings. And so on it goes. The people are being bound by private interpretation of scriptures by some who really don't have the welfare of their disciples at heart, but rather use them as pawns in their ambitious personal plans, propounded in the name of the Lord.

Beloved, we are called TO UNDO HEAVY BURDENS, TO LET THE OPPRESSED GO FREE, AND TO BREAK EVERY YOKE....THEN shall thy light break forth as the morning, and thine HEALTH shall spring forth speedily!


ISAIAH 58: 7
THE FAST OF THE LORD (Part 13)

IS IT NOT TO DEAL THY BREAD TO THE HUNGRY...

There is much to be said of how this great country takes responsibility in feeding the poor--not only at home but throughout the world; yet the hungry of the world remain in catastrophic statistics. There is an old proverb that says ":Give a man a fish and he will have a meal for a day; teach a man to fish and he will never go hungry."

Let us continue this commendable work; yet today I would suggest that we look at the spiritual side of this scripture, which is sadly neglected. You may disagree and say, "Why? We send out missionaries all over the world." Which we do. But let us ask what is the bread that is fed. Is it the bread of the doctrines of the organization with the intent of making disciples of the particular persuasion of the missionary? Concerning the Pharisees Jesus spoke on this issue in MATTHEW 23: 13-16. Woe unto you, scribes and Pharisees, hypocrites! For ye compass sea and land to make one proselyte, and when he is made, ye make him twofold more the child of hell than yourselves. (verse 15)

The world is crying out for the TRUE BREAD OF LIFE (JESUS) which is come down from heaven, not to be discipled into some Pharisaical organization. Even in this country as iniquity seems to abound everywhere, the great need today is the teaching of Jesus. We have majored in two aspects of Christianity--the Salvation Message of Heaven and Hell and the Personality of the Christ. In many cases, going to heaven for a problem free life has replaced the daily living of the TEACHING OF JESUS: Walking in forgiveness, loving our enemies, blessing those who curse us, doing good to them that hate us, and praying for those who despitefully use and persecute us. Strong words spoken by Jesus. Yet this is the bread that the world hungers for.

Is it not to deal thy bread to the hungry? What kind of bread do we give? Is it the bread of the Pharisees, or are we of those who give to the hungry Jesus, the bread of heaven come down! (JOHN 6: 32-35)

ISAIAH 58: 7

THE FAST OF THE LORD (Part 14)

A sign observed outside of a church in Florida read: If you are a drunk, a homosexual, a lesbian, a drug addict, a sinner of any kind, YOU ARE WELCOME HERE. My friend who told me this story said that immediately upon reading the sign a religious spirit rose up in self-righteous indignation within him, and he wanted to go in and straighten out the pastor. Then the Lord spoke to him and said, "Did I not come to seek and to save that which is lost?" My friend then told me how he had to repent of his hardened religious heart. He then went to a service in the church and found a happy redeemed 'mixed multitude' rejoicing and praising the Lord.

Back in Scotland, on one occasion a brother had a lapse and was found drinking alcohol. The 'Sanhedrin' council met and told him he couldn't come to church for a month! Did you ever hear of such 'bullbrown' hypocritical nonsense?! The delight of Jesus is in ministering to the poor that are cast out. He brought the poor that were cast out into His house. The scribes and Pharisees inquired of the disciples in MARK 2: 16--How is it that He eateth and drinketh with publicans and sinners?

One of the greatest stories ever told is the story of Jesus with the 'Woman at the Well'. In JOHN 3 Jesus instructs a religious leader that YOU MUST BE BORN AGAIN! To the woman at the well, He never mentioned salvation or her sin. He went straight to the crux of the problem--HER NEED FOR LIVING WATER. It is awesome to me that Jesus, the God of heaven, goes out of His way to bring to a Samaritan woman the message of JOHN 4: 14--WHOSOEVER DRINKETH OF THE WATER THAT I SHALL GIVE HIM SHALL NEVER THIRST. The people of Samaria saw a woman in sin; Jesus, the God of heaven manifested in flesh, saw A WOMAN IN NEED! And slaked her thirst. ---- Go ahead and shout! I'm shouting with you!

We used to sing a grand old anthem called *Room for Jesus, King of Glory*. Yet we will not have room for Jesus in the house of our hearts if we do not have room for the needy. It is time for us to bring the poor that are cast out into the house of our hearts!

THEN....the Lord shall guide thee continually.

ISAIAH 58: 7
THE FAST OF THE LORD (Part 15)

One of the seven abominations spoken of in PROVERBS 6: 17 is hands that shed innocent blood. I don't know about you, but I have been guilty of this down through my many years and still need the strength of the Lord not to kill with my tongue--or shed innocent blood. This is the same thought in ISAIAH where we are exhorted to cover our brother's nakedness. There is that something within us that takes pleasure in spreading filthy gossip, irrespective of whether it be true or otherwise.

If there be anything worse, I would suggest that it is when we break a confidence in the name of prayer for someone accused and we become the perpetuators of religious rumours. Remember...Jesus always stands on the side of the accused! Jesus died also for the one that is being exposed. There are those who, in the name of defending the Faith, are constantly accusing someone for some sort of indiscretion according to their very high hypocritical self-righteous holiness. When tongues are killing, nothing is sacred. Whether it be in the political, religious or domestic arena, nothing is spared. The joy of those telling tales is in someone's nakedness being uncovered.

There are those who will not only talk about their brother's nakedness, but in the bitterness of their mean soul they will strip him/her naked by false lies and made up stories to proudly vindicate their position...and, so tragic, often done in the name of their god. David said in PSALM 27: 12--

Deliver me not over unto the will of mine enemies: for false witnesses are risen up against me, and such as breathe out cruelty. I am ashamed to say that I've been there and done that. Only by God's Grace and Mercy has He covered me with His wings, hiding my nakedness from those who would have devoured my soul.

There are many destroyers out there who will have no mercy in their vicious religious attacks. They delight in exposing those who may have fallen by the way, who need their nakedness covered. May we be the Good Samaritan who will pour in the oil and wine of healing to those who have fallen into the hands of these thieves. As we cover our brother's nakedness....

THEN shall thy light break forth as the morning, AND THINE HEALTH SHALL SPRING FORTH SPEEDILY.

ISAIAH 58: 7
THE FAST OF THE LORD (Part 16)

Probably I have had more problems with this part of scripture than the rest in the Fast of the Lord. There is that vanity within that wants to be more important than who we really are in God's sight, and so we hide ourselves from our own fleshand seek to convince others how important we 'think' we are. Constantly I have run into those who, like myself, fool themselves, thinking that we are specially chosen for some great purpose. We are chosen as His servants for His praise and glory, yet some of us are constantly hiding the real truth of ourselves, cloaked under a covering of religious veneer, hoping to hit the religious big time!

I blush in remembrance of the first time, as a young preacher, I was allowed to sit at the table of the 'greats'. I had arrived at the first rung of the ladder of religious success. This continued for many years, clawing my way up that ladder, which was in essence a jungle of confusion...'dog eating dog!' You scratch my back and I'll scratch yours! Sadly, often having pleasure at some other preacher's failure...externally showing such concern, internally gloating, and always defending with indignant displeasure any who would seek to encroach on my 'territory'. Talk about the scribes and the Pharisees! They were potato pickers in comparison to my holier-than-thou religious self delusions of importance. Yet God in His great Love and Mercy began to show me that I really needed to be BORN AGAIN! I had been a Christian for many years with great outward show; but inside I was a whited sepulcher, a ravenous wolf, steeped in the arrogance of self-importance and, well...hiding from my own soulish flesh.

Jesus tells a beautiful story in LUKE 18: 10-14. The Pharisee prayed thanking God that he was not as other men were and went on to boast before the people how great he was. The publican couldn't lift his eyes to heaven as he smote his breast saying: God be merciful to me a sinner. Which of these two men went home justified?

When we come to that place in life where we recognize that we are no more special than anyone else, that we are all dependent on the Grace and Mercy of God, which is the great equalizer, no longer hiding ourselves from our own flesh...

THEN...THE LORD SHALL GUIDE THEE CONTINUALLY, AND SATISFY THY SOUL IN DROUGHT, AND MAKE FAT THY BONES.

ISAIAH 58: 9
THE FAST OF THE LORD (Part 17)

As I continue to write this series, I discover by repetition that the Truths of the Fast dominate much of my thinking and that there is a deep hunger within to walk into the authority of its message. Also, thinking in retrospect, having been in the ministry for many years I never once heard ISAIAH 58 referred too! Generally I spoke and listened to 'ear tickling messages' that sought to enhance the vanity of the minister, who so often sought to impress the audience with rhetoric and the profundity of his/her ability.

I ask myself today if I had been taught the Fast of the Lord as a young Christian and had applied it in my life, how many pitfalls would I have avoided? Also if I had ministered the Fast of the Lord instead of 'selfish escapism', would it have helped the sheep that I was given the responsibility to feed, helped them personally become more like Jesus both in walk and talk? If I had spoken less of my supposed insight on the 'hidden mysteries', less of the personality of Jesus and more of His MESSAGE, would it have effected greater Christ-like change in the hearers?

In verse 9 there are three critical aspects of Christ-like living that is sadly neglected today and also lacking in church teaching of today: If thou take away from the midst of thee the yoke, the putting forth of the finger, and speaking vanity. In many places the people are so yoked by Do's and Don'ts, so yoked financially and so scared by the fear of hell that they do not live Healthy Spiritual Lives. Their present
spiritual perspective generally contains only the view of a happy heavenly future, with little, if any, thought of spiritual growth and development in the here and now.

Pointing with the finger the faults and failures of others, whether true or false, has become an acceptable way of life, often spoken in self-righteous Vanity, as the accusers seek to establish their importance by exposing the supposed nakedness of others. We wonder why it seems that when we pray, the heavens are as brass and our prayers go unanswered! It is time for us to put away these abominations from our midst and THEN walk into
the Fast of the Lord.

THEN!------Then shalt thou call, and the Lord shall answer;

thou shalt cry, and He shall say, here I AM.

ISAIAH 58: 10
THE FAST OF THE LORD (Part 18)

So often we are hungry for revival or the blessing of the Lord, but we want it within the mindset of our particular religious persuasion...or 'Our Box'. Although denominationalism may tell you otherwise, many think that God is confined to the thinking or doctrinal statement of their particular 'box'. This goes back to the beginning when Cain KILLED his brother Abel over God's acceptance of the offered sacrifices. (Cain still kills today.)

In the time of the ministry of Jesus upon the earth, He reached out far beyond the limitations of the Jewish community, both in word and in deed. Wherever there was a hungry soul He was there to meet the need. As in the case of the Woman at the Well, Jesus gave this Samaritan woman the Bread and Water of Life which her soul yearned for. He satisfied a thirst that could not be quenched with multiple sexual relationships. Six times in the Gospels Jesus mentions non-Jewish places where it would be more tolerable in the day of Judgment than the places that refused to hear the message of the Gospel of the Kingdom...Tyre and Sidon, Syrian cities; and He even mentioned Sodom and Gomorrah being more acceptable than Capernaum.

Peter had problems about sharing his 'bread' with the

hungry Gentile household of Cornelius, and only at the promptings of Divine Visitation did he reluctantly proceed to fulfill his commission. (A thought---Peter wasn't too big to hold a house meeting!!!)

Twice in our chapter there is exhortation to reach out to the hungry, both in verse 7: To deal thy bread to the hungry. This is not only natural bread, but Spiritual Bread also, and in verses 10-11: And if thou draw out thy soul to the hungry, and satisfy the afflicted soul; THEN shall thy light rise in obscurity, and thy darkness be as the noon day: And the Lord shall guide thee continually, and satisfy thy soul in drought, and make fat thy bones: and thou shalt be like a watered garden, and like a spring of water, whose waters fail not.

The attributes declared by God in this chapter...Are not these the yearning of every hungry soul?

ISAIAH 58
THE FAST OF THE LORD (Part 19)

This chapter is a blueprint given in the Old Testament by God whereby wo/man can live full lives in relationship firstly with their brothers and sisters, then with God, and finally with him/herself. Since the beginning wo/man has struggled with moralities as the means of right relationships with God, but in our chapter it is made quite clear that right relationships and honorable communications with each other automatically opens the heart of God with the many THEN blessings. In the Living

Bible the interpreter gives a very practical insight into how we should conduct ourselves in our relationships with God and with mankind. Let me quote a portion of it:

Shout with the voice of a trumpet blast; tell My people of their sins! Yet they act so pious! They come to the temple every day and are so delighted to hear the reading of My laws---just as though they would obey them---just as though they don't despise the commandments of their God! How anxious they are to worship correctly; oh, how they love the temple services.

"We have fasted before You," they say. "Why aren't You impressed? Why don't You see our sacrifices? Why don't You hear our prayers? We have done much penance, and You don't even notice it!" God answers: I'll tell you why! Because you are living in evil pleasure even while you are fasting, and you keep right on oppressing your workers. Look, what good is fasting when you keep on fighting and quarreling? This kind of fasting will never get you anywhere with Me. Is this what I want---
this doing of penance and bowing like reeds in the wind and putting on sackcloth and covering yourselves with ashes?
Is this what you call fasting?

No, the kind of fast I want is that you stop oppressing those who work for you and treat them fairly and give them what they earn. I want you to share your food with the hungry and bring right into your own homes those who are helpless, poor and destitute. Clothe those who are cold and don't hide from relatives who need your help.

If you do these things, God will shed His own glorious light upon you. He will heal you; your godliness will lead you forward, and goodness will be a shield before you, and the glory of the Lord will protect you from behind. THEN, when you call, the Lord will answer. "Yes, I am here," He will quickly reply. All you need to do is to stop oppressing the weak, and to stop making false accusations and SPREADING VICIOUS RUMORS!

Feed the hungry! Help those in trouble! THEN your light will shine out from the darkness, and the darkness around you shall be as bright as day. And the Lord will guide you continually, and satisfy you with all good things, and keep you healthy too; and you will be like a well-watered garden, like an ever-flowing spring.

THE FAST OF THE LORD
(Part 20)

As we draw to the conclusion of this series, I ask myself if I have developed personal spiritual growth from having the honor from Father to share my thoughts with you. For myself, I have been taught the great need to be more respectful with my tongue in relationship with my brothers and sisters. A deeper awareness has developed as Jesus taught me that my thought life is where my problems arise, even as He taught that adultery in our thought life is in the eyes of God the same as the actual act. Bearing this in mind, the same must be true regarding evil thoughts toward others in situations that I might disagree with. Politically when I wish ill upon the President or any other elected official, I am actually seeking to impose my will upon the established mind of God. (Let every soul be subject unto the higher powers. For there is no power but of God: the powers that be are ordained of God. ROMANS 13: 1) Lies and untrue gossip against each other and willingly exposing the faults and failures of the weak are abominations unto the Lord.

Failure of repentance with no thought of restitution leaves one wide open to all manner of demonic influence and the diseases and sicknesses of Babylon. We cry unto God for revival and for Him to 'God bless America'; and He replies, "I want to! But you tie My hands by binding unforgiveness here upon earth; thus it is bound in heaven. Until you loose these things that you hold against each other upon the earth by forgiving, it cannot be loosed in heaven."

Salvation is a wonderful experience. But teaching that salvation and going to heaven (either by a rapture or by the grave) is all that is necessary has lulled many into a false sense of security, and the work of the 'Perfecting of the Saints' is totally disregarded. ISAIAH 58 and 1 CORINTHIANS 13 may seem like unattainable goals to many, yet God has given such scriptures as landmarks for each of us to strive toward so that we may fulfill our calling and walk here on earth as examples of the life of our Master...Jesus. As He is revealed in us, the world may then take thought.

Made in the USA
Coppell, TX
12 October 2021